# Little Pebble™

## All Kinds of Weather

# Sunny Weather

### A 4D BOOK

by Sally Lee

PEBBLE
a capstone imprint

## Download the Capstone  app!

- Ask an adult to download the Capstone 4D app.
- Scan the cover and stars inside the book for additional content.

When you scan a spread, you'll find fun extra stuff to go with this book! You can also find these things on the web at www.capstone4D.com using the password: sunny.01853

Little Pebble is published by Pebble
1710 Roe Crest Drive, North Mankato,
Minnesota 56003
www.mycapstone.com

**Library of Congress Cataloging-in-Publication Data**
is available on the Library of Congress website.

ISBN 978-1-9771-0185-3 (library binding)
ISBN 978-1-9771-0192-1 (paperback)
ISBN 978-1-9771-0198-3 (ebook pdf)

**Editorial Credits**
Marissa Kirkman, editor; Bobbie Nuytten, designer; Tracy Cummins, media researcher; Kris Wilfahrt, production specialist

**Photo Credits**
Shutterstock: Brian A Jackson, 11, Designer things, Design Element, Igor Kovalchuk, 13, liseykina, Cover, 1, Monkey Business Images, 21, Nikitina Olga, 12, Patrick Foto, 9, Pawel Kazmierczak, 17, Ruslan Merzliakov, 15 Bottom, S.Borisov, 5, sebikus, 7, Vibrant Image Studio, 15 Top, wowomnom, 18, XiXinXing, 19.

Printed and bound in the United States.
PA021

# Table of Contents

# Warm and Bright

The sky is blue.

There are no clouds.

It's sunny today.

# We Need the Sun

The sun is a giant star.
It is like a ball of fire.
The sun sends heat and
light to the earth.

We need the sun to live.

It makes our weather.

The sun warms the air.

Warm air meets cold air.

That makes wind.

The sun makes water evaporate.

The water turns into vapor.

This makes clouds.

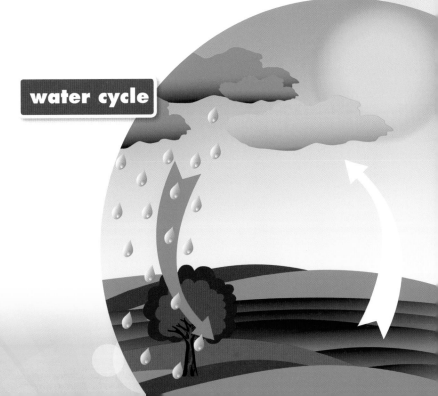

water cycle

The sun rises in the morning.

It brings light.

The sun sets in the evening.

This brings nighttime.

**sunrise**

**sunset**

# Warm or Cold?

Not all sunny days are warm.

A cold day can be sunny too.

Will today be warm or cold?

Check the forecast.

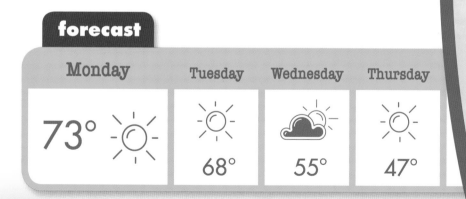

**forecast**

| Monday | Tuesday | Wednesday | Thursday |
|--------|---------|-----------|----------|
| 73° | 68° | 55° | 47° |

# Have Fun!

Ride your bike.

Feel the warm sun

on your skin.

Whee!

# Glossary

**cloud**—a white or gray mass of water droplets and dust in the air; raindrops form in certain types of clouds

**evaporate**—to change from a liquid to a gas

**forecast**—a report of future weather conditions

**heat**—a kind of energy that makes things hot or warm

**star**—a large ball of burning gases in space

**vapor**—a gas made from a liquid

**weather**—the condition outdoors at a certain time and place; weather changes with each season

# Read More

**Bauer, Marion Dane.** *Sun.* Weather Ready-to-Reads. New York: Simon Spotlight, 2016.

**De Seve, Karen.** *Little Kids First Big Book of Weather.* National Geographic Little Kids First Big Books. Washington, D.C.: National Geographic Kids, 2017.

**Rustad, Martha E. H.** *Today Is a Sunny Day.* What Is the Weather Today? North Mankato, Minn.: Capstone Press, 2017.

# Internet Sites

Use FactHound to find Internet sites related to this book.

Visit www.facthound.com

Just type in 9781977101853 and go.

**Super-cool stuff!** Check out projects, games and lots more at **www.capstonekids.com**

# Critical Thinking Questions

1. What is the sun?

2. How does the sun help to make clouds?

3. What does the weather feel like on a sunny day?

# Index